Collins
INTERNATIONAL PRIMARY ENGLISH

Workbook 5

William Collins' dream of knowledge for all began with the publication of his first book in 1819.
A self-educated mill worker, he not only enriched millions of lives, but also founded a flourishing publishing house.
Today, staying true to this spirit, Collins books are packed with inspiration, innovation and practical expertise. They place you at the centre of a world of possibility and give you exactly what you need to explore it.

Collins. Freedom to teach.

Published by Collins
An imprint of HarperCollins*Publishers*
The News Building
1 London Bridge Street
London SE1 9GF

1st Floor, Watermarque Building, Ringsend Road, Dublin 4, Ireland

Browse the complete Collins catalogue at www.collins.co.uk

ISBN 978-0-00-836773-2

British Library Cataloguing-in-Publication Data
A catalogue record for this publication is available from the British Library.

Authors: Jan Gallow and (1st edition) Fiona MacGregor
Series editor: Daphne Paizee
Publisher: Elaine Higgleton
Product developer: Natasha Paul
Project manager: Karen Williams
Development editor: Sonya Newland
Copyeditor: Karen Williams
Proofreader: Catherine Dakin
Cover designer: Gordon MacGilp
Cover illustrator: Emma Chichester Clark
Internal designer and typesetter: Ken Vail Graphic Design Ltd.
Text permissions researcher: Rachel Thorne
Image permissions researcher: Alison Prior
Illustrators: Ken Vail Graphic Design Ltd., Advocate Art, Beehive Illustration and QBS Learning
Production controller: Lyndsey Rogers
Printed in Great Britain by Martins the Printers

Third-party websites, publications and resources referred to in this publication have not been endorsed by Cambridge Assessment International Education.

With thanks to the following teachers and schools for reviewing materials in development: Amanda DuPratt, Shreyaa Dutta Gupta, Sharmila Majumdar, Sushmita Ray and Sukanya Singhal, Calcutta International School; Akash Raut, DSB International School, Mumbai; Melissa Brobst, International School of Budapest; Shalini Reddy, Manthan International School; Taman Rama Intercultural School.

Contents

1 What's your name?

Talk about what you think happens next in Chapter 1 of *Saffy's Angel*.

What doesn't Saffron know?

Complete this spider diagram by filling in your ideas.

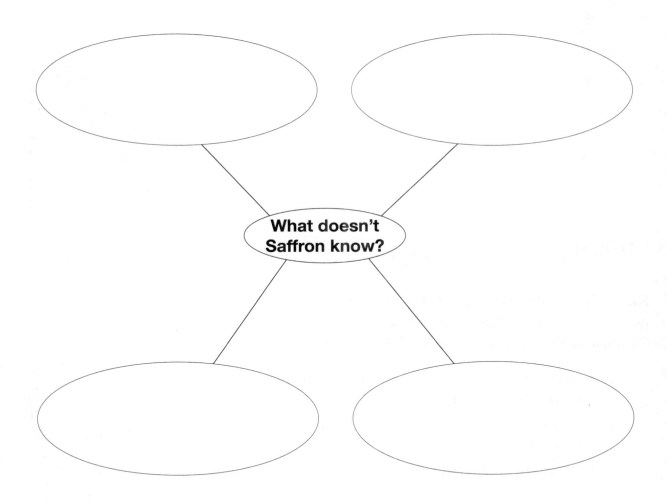

Student's Book pages 1–3

Reread the text from *Saffy's Angel*. What do you think will happen next? Write the next paragraph.

Doesn't Saffron know?

Nouns Student's Book pages 4–5

Read the sentences. Underline the countable nouns and circle the uncountable nouns. Complete the sentences with *fewer* or *less*.

a There were _____ yellow squares than red squares on the chart.

b There was _____ coal in the bucket than on the rug.

c The health visitor had _____ children than Mrs Casson.

d They owned _____ stable chairs than wobbly chairs.

e The hamster had _____ paint on its feet than the health visitor's notes.

The nouns in the sentences below are in the singular form. Write the sentences so that all the nouns are in the plural form.

a The child played the cello.

_____

_____

b The shepherd protected the calf from the wolf.

_____

_____

c The cliff they climbed were steep.

_____

_____

d "You have many book on your shelf," she said.

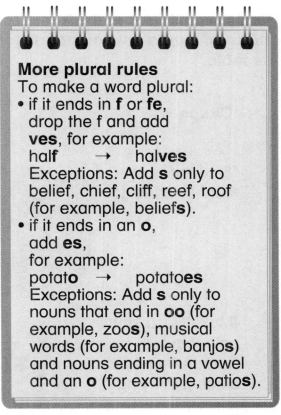

More plural rules
To make a word plural:
• if it ends in **f** or **fe**, drop the f and add **ves**, for example:
half → hal**ves**
Exceptions: Add **s** only to belief, chief, cliff, reef, roof (for example, belief**s**).
• if it ends in an **o**, add **es**, for example:
potat**o** → potato**es**
Exceptions: Add **s** only to nouns that end in **oo** (for example, zoo**s**), musical words (for example, banjo**s**) and nouns ending in a vowel and an **o** (for example, patio**s**).

_____

_____

e He filled up the box with paint can.

_____

_____

f We gave the key to the guy at the shop.

_____

g "Do you have any potato and tomato?" he asked.

_____

h You will catch more fish at the reef.

_____

Student's Book pages 1–3

Read the dialogue in the table from *Saffy's Angel*. What does the writer's choice of words tell you about each character? Write your ideas in the table.

Dialogue	What the dialogue tells me about the character
"Find the baby first," said Indigo.	
"Make Rose shut up!" shouted Saffron from her stool. "I'm trying to read!"	
"Saffron reads anything now!" the children's mother told the health visitor, proudly.	
"Very nice!" the health worker replied. "My twins were fluent readers at four years old."	

Vocabulary

Student's Book pages 4–5

Draw lines to match the colourful expressions to their meanings.

to feel blue	in a bad mood
to see red	very angry
to feel green	cowardly
to be yellow	feeling sick
to be in a black mood	feeling sad

Punctuation

Student's Book page 8

All the punctuation has been lost from the story! Add the correct punctuation to the paragraph.

in the car as we started our long journey to Lewiston in Idaho my grandmother hiddle said Salamanca why don't you entertain us

gramps said yes tell us a story

instantly phoebe winterbottom came to mind

1 **Read the text about naming children. Then answer the questions.**

Things that happen when a child is born often influence the name that is given to the child. One little girl was called **Caroline** because she was born in the middle of a power cut and as the power came back on, *Sweet Caroline* was being played on the radio. Another girl was called **Sirene** because she was born during an air raid and the siren was heard soon afterwards.

Some names relate to the time of birth – **Noel**, **April**, **June** and **May**, for example.

Less poetic is the story reported in an American newspaper to the effect that a baby boy had just been named **Bill** "because he came on the last day of the month". This is traditionally the day when people have to pay their bills for the month!

a What is *Sweet Caroline*?

_____

b How did Sirene get her name?

_____

c What day do you think Noel was born on?

_____

d Where does Bill live?

_____

e What name would you give a baby that was born:

- during a hurricane? _____

- on a camping trip? _____

- at sea? _____

- when the Olympic Games were taking place? _____

2 Do some research to find out where the names in the chart below come from and what they mean. If you are not able to look up the meanings, invent your own.

Name	From which country?	Meaning
Chandra		
Xiong		
Zainab		
Stephen		
Dermot		

3 Write your own collective nouns for the words below. Have fun!

a a _____ of sisters

b a _____ of pigeons

c a _____ of books

d a _____ of bad ideas

e a _____ of friends

f a _____ of dirty clothes

g a _____ of computers

h a _____ of teachers

i a _____ of memories

j a _____ of dancers

1 **Answer the questions about the poem. You will need to do research.**

a What does the name 'Hiawatha' mean?

_____

b Who wrote the poem?

_____

c When was the poem published?

_____

d Which culture is the poem about?

_____

e What style of poem is it?

_____

2 **Read the poem and answer the questions.**

a What type of person is Hiawatha? Give reasons for your answer.

_____

b What gives the poem rhythm?

_____

c Which words in the poem influence your opinion of Iagoo? Why?

_____

d Does Hiawatha like animals? How do you know?

_____

e Do the animals trust Hiawatha? How do you know?

_____

_____

f What do you think happens next?

_____

_____

2 Strange school stories

1 Study the advertisement below.

Just bring in this coupon
before 10 February for your
tastebud explosion!!

Paolo's Pizzas!!!

Home of the famous
'Funghirama'

Delicious mounds of melted
cheese, and roasty-toasty
mushrooms

And now, a mouth-watering
25 per cent off!

25% off at Paolo's Pizzas!

a Find and underline all the adjectives.

b What effect do all these adjectives have on you, as the reader?

_____

_____

c What kind of language is used in the text?

_____

_____

d What is the purpose of using this kind of language in this text?

_____

_____

2 Look at the drawings of two schools below. Give each school a name. Make up a motto for each school.

School name:

School motto:

School name:

School motto:

Vocabulary Student's Book pages 16–18

Using school as the root word, create a spider diagram of words and phrases that include 'school'.

Student's Book pages 16–17

1 List things you love and don't love about school.

Things I love about school	Things I don't love about school

2 Find and correct the seven errors in the sentences below. Rewrite the sentences correctly.

a Louis thourght for a minute. He did'nt want the man distributing the children.

_____

_____

b He told the man she was Mrs Jewls. he took the package. It wayed alot.

_____

_____

Pronouns   Student's Book pages 26–27

1 Use the pronouns in the box to complete the sentences.

| you | he | mine | yours | him | he | I | them |

Jabu looked at the two pairs of shoes. "Which pair is _____ and

which is _____?" _____ asked.

"_____ don't know," Lucia replied.

"These are my shoes," Jordan said, picking

_____ up. "_____ two can fight about the others."

Lucia looked at _____.

_____ avoided her eyes and ran off.

2 Say what kind of pronoun each of the answers in question 1 was.

_____   _____

_____   _____

_____   _____

_____   _____

3 Read the notes about possessive pronouns. Look at the table you completed in activity 3 on page 27 of your Student's Book. Can you see that all of the examples in the third column are possessive pronouns?

Write a list of all the possessive pronouns.

_____   _____

_____   _____

_____   _____

_____   _____

Possessive pronouns show when something belongs to someone.
For example: This is **mine**.
That is **his**.
Those books are **theirs**.

Can you see that **theirs** tells you the books belong to **them**?

4 Complete the poem below with possessive pronouns.

I want my lunch. It's _____, the baby cried.

That's not _____, it's mine, the boy lied.

It's not our turn, it's _____, the players replied.

You've had a break, now we need _____, the teachers sighed.

Decide how to present *Falling asleep in class*. Talk about the questions below and write notes.

a Will everyone speak at once or will you take turns? What will sound best?

_____

_____

_____

b Will you vary the volume and speed? How and when?

_____

_____

_____

c How will you use expression? Which words need extra expression?

_____

_____

_____

d Are you going to act out what happens? Apart from speaking, what other things can you do to communicate?

_____

_____

_____

e Will you wear costumes and use props? If so, what do you need?

_____

_____

_____

3 Hair-raising stories

Adverbs Student's Book pages 29–30

1 **Complete the chart below of adverbs of comparison.**

fast	faster	fastest
high		
	lower	
		slowest
	quicker	
		hardest
loud		
	softer	

2 **Use the adverbs in the chart and other adverbs you may know to complete the paragraph below.**

In our family Shamila is the _____,

as she always takes forever to finish things.

Ismael is the _____ because

his voice is just, well, very loud. I am

_____ than Shamila at finishing

things and _____ than Ismael

when I speak, and because I try my _____ at school I am the

_____ in our family.

Write in the dialogue for the cartoon boxes about the folk tale
Why women have long hair.

Vocabulary   Student's Book pages 31–34

1 **Below are some proverbs. Write down what you think the meaning of each proverb is.**

a All that glitters is not gold.

_____

b The apple doesn't fall far from the tree.

_____

c A bird in the hand is worth two in the bush.

_____

d Never look a gift horse in the mouth.

_____

e Too many cooks spoil the broth.

_____

f You can't judge a book by its cover.

_____

g Curiosity killed the cat.

_____

2 **Answer the questions below.**

a Which proverb from the list do you think suits the Nigerian folk tale best? Explain why.

_____

_____

b Write your own proverb for this story. Say what it means and how it fits the folk tale.

_____

_____

3 You know that suffixes are word endings.

Add suffixes to the words in the box to make new words. How many new words can you make with each root word?

care	child	parent
rely	free	king
neighbour	truth	beauty

Suffixes
–ful means full of
–able / –ible means able to
–less means without
–hood means a state of
–dom makes a noun abstract

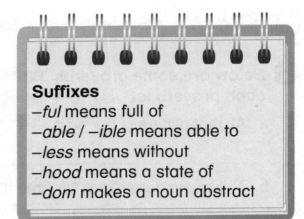

18

Read the text below from an encyclopedia. Then answer the questions.

HAIR

The hairs on mammals have two main functions. The first is to do with controlling body temperature. Mammals have a steady, warm body temperature. To be able to keep this up they have to make sure that heat does not escape from the body too fast.

When you are cold the hairs on your body stand up, trapping the warm air between them in an effort to keep up your body temperature. This is called getting 'goosebumps'. In animals the hairs form an insulating and waterproof coat that slows down heat loss.

The second function of hair is to give each mammal its own distinctive markings. These are hairs of different colours and lengths. Even we have different hair types.

a Scan the text. What are the two main functions of hair?

_____

_____

b What feature mentioned in the text is common to all mammals?

_____

_____

c Describe how goosebumps form.

_____

_____

d Describe your own 'distinctive markings'. What do you look like? Mention other features aside from hair.

_____

_____

Student's Book pages 31–37

PAIR WORK. Complete the chart to show what is similar and what is different about the two stories you read in Unit 3. Use the headings as a guideline.

Features	Why women have long hair	Rapunzel
Where the story is from		
Main character		
Person telling the story (character, narrator, and so on)		
Situation/what the story is about		
What the main character does 'wrong'		
How she is 'punished'		
The resolution at the end		
Moral of the story		
My own opinion of the story		

4 Reading a classic: *Alice in Wonderland*

Writing Student's Book page 44

1 **Complete the paragraphs by using words from the box.**

stage	props	lighting	actors	backstage
costume	stage manager	director	cues	rehearsals

Many people work _____ to create a performance.

The _____ is in charge and he or she tells the _____ how to say their lines and how to move on stage.

However, the organisation behind the curtains is the _____'s responsibility. She gives actors their _____ which tells them when it is time to go on _____. She also organises _____ and makes sure that the correct _____ and costumes are used at the right time.

The person in charge of _____ creates the mood of the play. He can use spotlights to follow an actor or stage lights to imitate day and night.

The _____ manager decides what the characters will wear in each scene.

2 **What backstage role would you be best at and why? Write a paragraph explaining your choice.**

_____

_____

_____

_____

_____

_____

1 **Read the words below.**

forest ☐

chorus ☐

lull ☐

slumber ☐

gigantic ☐

exit ☐

magical ☐

thee ☐

tryst ☐

troop ☐

bewilderment ☐

savage ☐

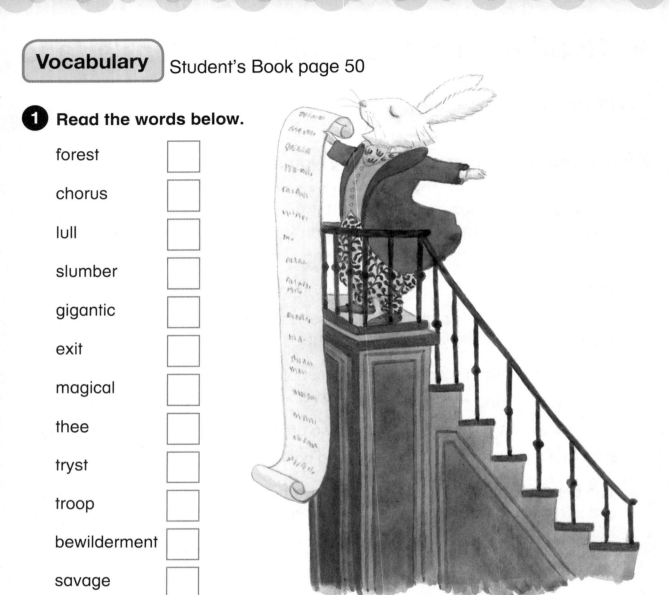

a Number the words in the box in alphabetical order.

b Read the words in the context of the play. Tell your partner what you think each word means.

c Look up the meaning of each word in a dictionary to see if your meaning was correct.

2 **Find and circle the words in the word search.**

tryst	gigantic	troop	thee	forest	lull
bewilderment	slumber	exit	savage	chorus	magical

x	m	a	g	i	c	a	l	k	v	u	v
b	s	r	i	v	h	q	z	q	j	t	f
s	a	h	g	e	o	y	z	d	i	c	o
l	v	g	a	t	r	o	o	p	l	o	r
u	a	l	n	z	u	f	j	t	h	e	e
m	g	q	t	k	s	q	t	l	k	g	s
b	e	w	i	l	d	e	r	m	e	n	t
e	f	d	c	u	q	x	y	a	v	y	q
r	p	k	v	l	c	i	s	c	w	j	k
g	p	w	s	l	l	t	t	a	m	p	q

3 **Write two complete sentences using some of the words from the word search in activity 2.**

_____

_____

_____

_____

**Listen carefully to the strange experience Alice has at a tea party.
Number the events below so they are in the correct order.**

The March Hare asks Alice to tell a story. ☐

The Hatter asks a riddle. ☐

The March Hare and the Hatter try to put the Dormouse in a teapot. ☐

The Hatter tells them to move round the table. ☐

Alice sees the March Hare, the Hatter and the Dormouse at a table set for tea. ☐

Alice sits down at the table to have tea. ☐

The Dormouse begins to tell a story about three sisters. ☐

The March Hare dips his watch in the tea. ☐

Alice notices a little door in a tree. ☐

The Hatter tells Alice she needs a haircut. ☐

The Hatter sings a rhyme. ☐

They tell Alice there is no room for her at the table. ☐

1 **Draw your favourite character from the film.**

2 **Write about your character. Use complete sentences.**

My favourite character is _____ because _____

_____

_____

_____

_____

_____

_____

Direct and reported speech — Student's Book pages 52–53

1 **Change the sentences below from reported speech to direct speech.**

For example:

She said that she wanted to be an actor when she grew up.

She said, "I want to be an actor when I grow up."

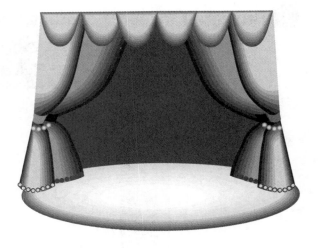

a Dennis said that he wanted to do the sound effects.

_____

_____

b The teacher said that he was allowed to be loud.

_____

_____

c Tharlikha said that she was going to be the costume director.

_____

_____

d Her mother asked if she wanted to borrow her old cloak.

_____

_____

e Miriam said that she was going to be a famous movie star one day.

_____

_____

2 **Change the sentences below from direct speech to reported speech. Remember to change the time words too.**

For example:

Sipho asked, "Can I bring my costume to school tomorrow?"

Sipho asked if he could bring his costume to school the next day.

a The teacher said, "Mary, make sure all the props are here tomorrow."

_____

_____

b Jose said, "We will practise our play today, at lunchtime."

_____

_____

c Ronda asked, "When is the next rehearsal?"

_____

_____

d The Stage Manager said, "It is at the same time as the one yesterday."

_____

_____

e The teacher asked, "Are you all ready for opening night tomorrow?"

_____

_____

Add speech marks to the sentences below. Fill the gaps with words from the box.

exclaimed	muttered	announced	asked
cried	replied	explained	complained

a The interviewer _____, What actually happened that day?

b Alice _____, While I was out walking, I came across a tea party.

c The Mad Hatter and March Hare _____, No room! No room! as they saw Alice coming.

d There's plenty of room! _____ Alice.

e I don't like your hair. It needs to be cut, _____ the Hatter.

f Well, I don't like rude people, _____ Alice under her breath.

g When I sang to the Queen, she threatened to cut off my head, _____ the Hatter.

h It's time to move round! _____ the Hatter.

5 Songs of the sea

Vocabulary Student's Book page 55

Below is the thesaurus entry you find if you look up the word 'twist'.

wriggle *v* **1** = **crawl**, jerk, jiggle, slink, snake, squirm, turn, twist, waggle, wiggle, worm, writhe, zigzag **2** = **manoeuvre**, dodge, extricate oneself ▷ *n* **3** = **twist**, jerk, jiggle, squirm, turn, waggle, wiggle

a Under what headword do you find 'twist'? _____

b What do you think the letters *v* and *n* mean? _____

c What do the numbers 1, 2 and 3 mean? _____

d Look up one of the synonyms for 'twist' in the dictionary and write down its definition.

_____

_____

_____

e Which words do you particularly like? Write sentences that include the words.

_____

_____

_____

Use the outline below to help you prepare your point of view for the debate.

Remember

Make notes.

Write key words, not sentences.

Note down several different arguments to support your point of view.

Find reasons to back each argument.

If possible, do research to find facts and figures to back up your point of view.

Introduction: state your point of view.

Argument 1	Argument 2	Argument 3

Conclusion: restate your point of view.

1 **Find the subject, verb and object in the sentences below. Underline the verb in red, circle the subject in green and circle the object in blue.**

a Whales are huge mammals.

b They sing strange and beautiful songs.

c Kahu's great-grandfather did not like new traditions.

d Her cousin watched the helicopters.

e Many New Zealanders have seen the movie.

f The movie won three international awards.

2 **Use the connectives in the box to join the simple sentences.**

and	but	or

a We heard the news. We went to the beach.

_____

b Everyone was there. It was raining.

_____

c We stared out to sea. We couldn't see her at first.

_____

d She could have stayed on the beach. She could have gone into the sea.

_____

e She was a good swimmer. He was a good swimmer.

_____

f She rode on the whale. She went out to sea.

_____

32

Writing Student's Book pages 55–56 and 62–63

Read all the texts from *The Whale Rider* in the Student's Book. Think about how these parts of the story were shown in the film. Complete the chart below to compare the film to the text.

The Whale Rider	How does the film compare to the text?
The whales in text 1	
The whales in text 2	
The setting in text 1	
The setting in text 2	
Kahu in text 2	
The plot (story line)	

Reading Student's Book page 64

Read the poem *Sea Fever*. Then answer the questions below.

    a Write down the rhyming words at the end of each line.

_____

_____

_____

_____

    b Find an example of alliteration in line 3.

_____

_____

    c Find another example of alliteration anywhere in the poem.

_____

_____

    d What does the poet mean by 'the lonely sea'?

_____

_____

    e What is the wind compared to in verse 3? Why do you think the poet chose to compare the wind to this?

_____

_____

    f Underline the theme of the poem.

       A longing to be at the beach.

       A longing for freedom and adventure.

       A longing to go sailing.

1 **Read the poem below.**

The sea

Crashing and smashing
Freezing cold raging huge swells
Not inviting me

Haiku is a short Japanese poem that is usually about nature. It has:

- 3 lines that usually do not rhyme.

- 17 syllables in total.

- 5 syllables in the first and third lines.

- 7 syllables in the second line.

2 **Write a haiku. Use words that create feeling and mood.**

_____

_____

_____

_____

_____

3 **Compare the poems _The Sea_ and _Sea Fever_.**

	The Sea	_Sea Fever_
Theme		
Setting		
Structure		
Rhythm		
Rhyme		

6 Stories from around the world

1 Use the prefixes in the box to make as many new words as you can from the roots on the word tree.

bi–	un–	im–	co–	ex–

perfect

happy

focal

proper

operate

president

pilot

cycle

expected

possible

_____

_____

_____

_____

_____

2 **Complete the words from *Walk Two Moons*. Write the correct word next to the matching clue.**

contin__ __ d	sh__wl	tre__ __ling
blu__ __ing	cur__ __ sity	plag__ __

a _____ a piece of clothing worn to cover the head and shoulders

b _____ to become red in the face

c _____ a desire to know something

d _____ started speaking again

e _____ an epidemic disease

f _____ to shake a little, uncontrollably

3 **Look at the example and then complete the diagram.**

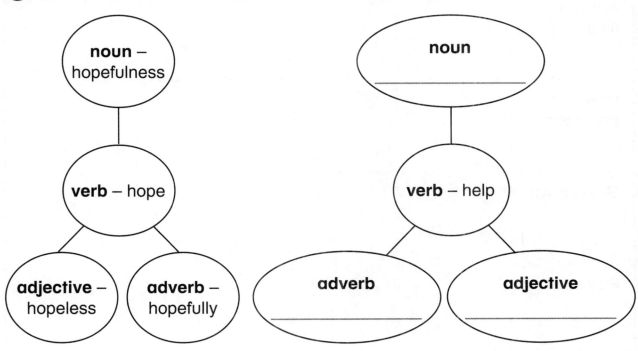

noun –
hopefulness

verb – hope

adjective –
hopeless

adverb –
hopefully

noun
_____

verb – help

adverb
_____

adjective
_____

Would you like to receive Pandora's gifts? Give a reason for your choice.

Gifts	Yes or No	Reason
Fancy shawl		
Silver dress		
Beauty		
Ability to sing		
Power of persuasion		
Gold crown		
Flowers		

1 **Look at each sentence below. Colour the main clause in red and the subordinate clause in blue. Circle the connective in green.**

a I love this story because it is funny.

b Salamanca uses big words when she wants to impress her friends.

c Although Ben gets irritated with Phoebe, they are still friends.

d Phoebe goes red when she gets embarrassed.

e Mr Birkway disagreed with Phoebe, although he didn't stop her from talking.

f The class was listening because the story was interesting.

2 **Draw a line to match the beginning of each sentence to the correct conjunction. Then correct the subordinate clause.**

Something good might happen	although	he kept interrupting.
Phoebe was irritated with Ben	so	that is why there is hope.
My heart stopped racing	after	I started distracting her.
My lip was no longer trembling	because	the first two sentences.
I was bored listening to Phoebe	so	I still felt nervous.

1 List the good and bad gifts that Pandora received.

Good gifts	Bad gifts

2 PAIR WORK. Talk about your list. Rank the gifts from best to worst.

Student's Book pages 72–74

1 Find and write down details from the story that give you information about:

a how Anansi treats other animals.

_____

_____

b what Anansi thinks about himself.

_____

_____

c what Anansi does when he does not get his own way.

_____

_____

2 Complete the spider diagram by writing words that describe Anansi.

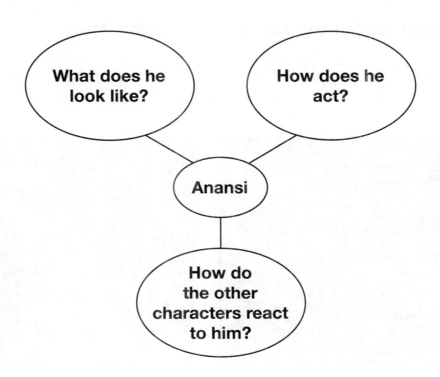

3 **Compare the characters of Firefly and Tiger.**

   a How are they the same?

_____

_____

   b How are they different?

_____

_____

4 **Compare the characters of Tiger and Anansi.**

   a How are they the same?

_____

_____

   b How are they different?

_____

_____

5 **Describe the relationship between Anansi and Horse.**

_____

_____

7 Exploring space

When making notes you only need to write key words. Key words are the words that highlight the main points.

1 Read the paragraphs below about how astronauts live in space. Underline the key words.

> Gravity gets less and less as you move further from Earth, and if you get far enough away you become weightless and you float.
>
> Astronauts eat food from sealed containers and they put the empty packets into a special bin afterwards. They can't put salt and pepper on their food because the salt and pepper floats away!
>
> When astronauts need to sleep they tie themselves down, otherwise they could float around and bump into things. They usually sleep in sleeping bags.

2 Now complete the spider diagram to make short notes about the information.

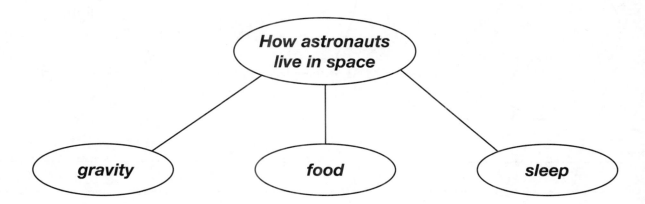

1 Use the subordinate clauses below in sentences of your own.

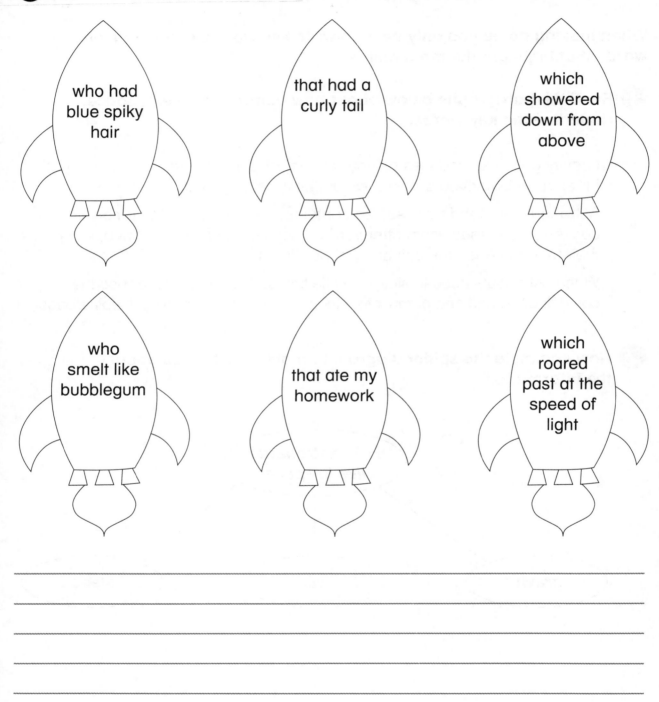

who had blue spiky hair

that had a curly tail

which showered down from above

who smelt like bubblegum

that ate my homework

which roared past at the speed of light

_____

_____

_____

_____

_____

_____

2 Add 'who', 'whom', 'which' or 'that' to the sentences below.

a My friend, _____ lives next door, believes in aliens.

b She says her rabbit, _____ she got from the petshop, is a space creature.

c The rabbit, _____ dug a hole under our fence, is crazy, but I don't think _____ he is an alien.

d Her house, _____ looks like ours on the outside, is very different inside.

e The hallway, _____ is very dark, is painted purple.

f Her granny, _____ lives with them, has a chair in the corner.

g She is one of twenty-four people _____ live in the house.

h It makes our house, _____ I like, feel quite empty.

Vocabulary Student's Book page 80

Find and circle all the space words from the box in this word search. Use the words to write an information paragraph about space.

dimension

space

moon

sun

orbit

energy

weight

a	s	t	r	o	n	a	u	t	p
d	p	a	n	r	o	n	u	s	s
i	a	m	p	b	i	n	t	e	w
m	c	h	l	i	g	h	t	n	e
e	e	a	r	t	h	x	i	e	i
n	o	o	y	t	i	v	a	r	g
s	t	f	o	r	c	e	s	g	h
i	t	r	a	v	e	l	f	y	t
o	t	a	o	l	f	c	e	i	p
n	o	o	m	p	t	r	a	c	e
p	m	o	o	d	i	o	v	o	g

Answer the questions below about the two texts on Student's Book pages 81 and 82. Then look at the what is the same and what is different between the two texts.

Features	A Wrinkle in Time	The speed of light
What is the type of text?		
What is the purpose?		
What style of writing is used?		
Is the text formal or infomal?		
How is the text organised?		
What is your opinion of the text?		

1 **Complete the chart below about the two poems.**

Features	Space is like a place so big and huge that my small brain can't really understand it the vast and open sky oh wow oh why	Space is like the deepest sea with not enough air for you and me people in space always float around but we like to stay on the ground
Theme What is the main idea?		
Form How are the poems set out? How many lines do they have?		
Word choice How does the poet's choice of words create mood and feeling?		
Tone How do the poets express themselves? For example, is the tone humorous, serious, admiring?		
Opinion What do you think of each poem? Which do you prefer?		

2 Imagine that you wrote the poems on page 47. You are editing your poems to change and add figures of speech. Write your ideas in the chart below. Describe what the figure of speech means.

My ideas	What does this mean?
Simile to describe 'space'	
Metaphor to describe 'space'	
Simile to describe 'brain'	
Metaphor to describe 'ground'	
Personification to describe 'sky'	

8 Here is the news

Vocabulary Student's Book pages 87–91

1 Complete the chart below about the word 'broadcast'.

BROADCAST		
Dictionary definition	**Meaning in my own words**	**Word in a sentence**

2 Complete the sentences below with 'should', 'would' or 'could'. There is more than one modal verb that can be used in some sentences.

a If you know the rules, you _____ obey them.

b If I was a paddler, I _____ be more careful.

c If I was you, I _____ call Sea Rescue to help.

d They _____ have warned you not to go paddling in that huge surf.

e We decided that we _____ paddle on Tuesday.

f He _____ win an award for his good deed.

g _____ you not wear a life jacket, your life may be at risk.

h Anything _____ have happened if Sea Rescue hadn't responded quickly.

1 Write an answer to each of the following
questions. Begin your answer with 'yes'
or 'no' and include a contraction.

For example: **Is it bad news?**

Yes, it's bad news.

a Can I turn off the radio?

_____

b Will he come to the prize-giving?

_____

c Would you wear a life jacket?

_____

d Can you write a report for us?

_____

e Should I visit him in hospital?

_____

f Could he have been more careful?

_____

g Will you call Sea Rescue?

_____

h Are they on their way to save him?

_____

i Are you going to help them?

_____

2 **Complete both of the charts below.**

I am	I'm
they have	
you are	
we shall	
must not	
will not	
should have	

I have	I've
	they'll
	you'd
	we're
	wouldn't
	can't
	would've

3 **Put the apostrophes in the correct places in the sentences below.**

a Shes coming to town to see her friends sister.

b Theyre going to watch the movie about Shauns sheep

c I cant believe theyd watch such rubbish.

d Its her friends turn to choose; next time, she chooses.

e Well, I hope they go to a girls movie then.

1 GROUP WORK. Read the poem below aloud.

Bad News Blues

It's all bad, isn't it?
what you read in the news—
Man Murders Wife
Home Affairs Queues
Miners On Strike
Town Council Sues—
It's all bad, isn't it?
what you read in the news.

I want to read good things,
like Man Rescues Shark,
or People Applaud
When Town Opens Park,
or Girl Rescues Child
Afraid of the Dark,
or what about Dog
Saves Them All with One Bark?

Perhaps we should have
two newspapers each day.
If you want doom and gloom,
why then, you have to pay!
But if you prefer the good
news – you're like me –
And we'll get our newspapers
completely free.

Read all about it!

2 Which lines rhyme in each verse?

3 **Answer the questions below.**

a Why do so many of the words in the first two verses have capital letters?

_____

b Which article would you like to read? Explain why.

_____

_____

c Which words rhyme with: down, fan and zoom?

_____

_____

_____

d Imagine that you are the poet. Write a last line for verse 3. Your line must end with the words 'isn't it?'.

_____

_____

4 **Write eye-catching and interesting news headlines in the boxes.**

```
┌─────────────────────────────────────────┐
│                                         │
│                                         │
│                                         │
│                                         │
└─────────────────────────────────────────┘
```

```
┌─────────────────────────────────────────┐
│                                         │
│                                         │
│                                         │
└─────────────────────────────────────────┘
```

```
┌─────────────────────────────────────────┐
│                                         │
│                                         │
│                                         │
└─────────────────────────────────────────┘
```

9 Our changing Earth

Vocabulary Student's Book pages 103–106

1 **Read the words in the word cloud.**

Africa

drought

equator

jungle

savannah

floods

greenhouse

carbon dioxide

desert

continent

a Put the words into alphabetical order.

_____

_____

_____

_____

_____

_____

_____

_____

_____

b Read the words in context in your Student's Book.

Look up the meanings of the words you do not understand and write them in your spelling log.

2 **Complete the sentences with words from the box.**

> faster   harder   hotter   drier
>
> older   smaller   weaker

a Our weather is getting _____ .

b It means it's getting _____ to predict.

c When I get _____ I'll build my house on high ground.

d When hurricanes reach land they get _____ .

e Mudslides are dangerous because they travel
much _____ than anyone can run.

f We're trying to make our carbon footprint
_____ by walking to school.

g Some places are getting _____
while others are getting wetter.

3 The sentences below come from the texts on pages 106 and 107 of the Student's Book. Draw lines to match the beginning of the sentence to the end.

I'll tie ropes along the road, so that people   (1)   (a)   know when they're in danger.

I'll build my house on high ground   (2)   (b)   much rain to grow.

I'll plant   (3)   (c)   so that water doesn't come in.

I'll plant crops that don't need   (4)   (d)   can see them even in a flood.

I'll make houses that don't break up   (5)   (e)   more trees.

I'll make sure that people   (6)   (f)   when hurricanes come.

4 **Match the children with their speech bubbles.**

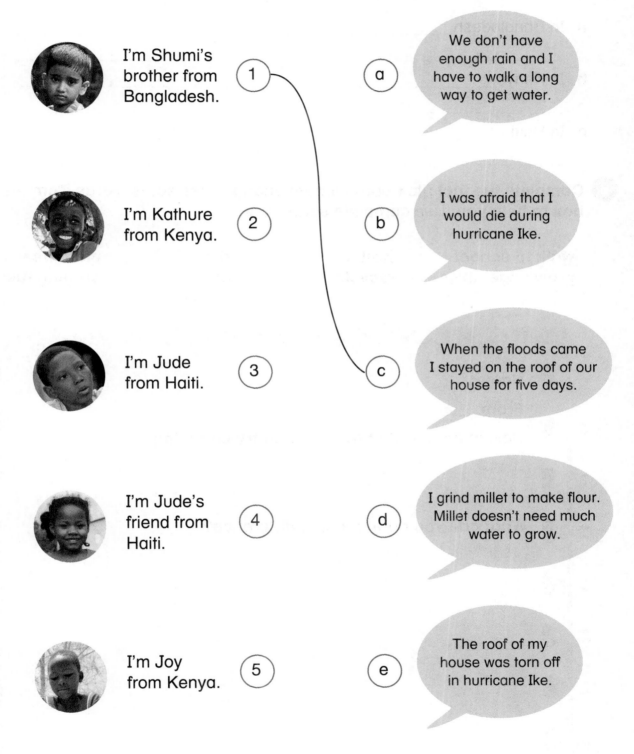

I'm Shumi's brother from Bangladesh. ①

I'm Kathure from Kenya. ②

I'm Jude from Haiti. ③

I'm Jude's friend from Haiti. ④

I'm Joy from Kenya. ⑤

ⓐ We don't have enough rain and I have to walk a long way to get water.

ⓑ I was afraid that I would die during hurricane Ike.

ⓒ When the floods came I stayed on the roof of our house for five days.

ⓓ I grind millet to make flour. Millet doesn't need much water to grow.

ⓔ The roof of my house was torn off in hurricane Ike.

5 Complete the sentences below. Say what is happening in each country because of climate change.

a In Bangladesh _____

_____

b In Kenya _____

_____

c In Haiti _____

_____

6 Complete the fact file about climate change. Use some words from the box to help you. Use complete sentences.

walk to school	wetter	drier	plant trees
grow vegetables	recycle	hotter	burning fuel

Name: _____

From: _____

How is the weather in your country changing? _____

_____

_____

What can you do to make a difference? _____

_____

_____

_____

_____

_____

7 Complete the table of comparative adjectives.

Adjective	Comparative	Superlative
high		
	sadder than	
		the oldest
long		
		the hungriest
much		
	darker than	
	more scared than	
		the most afraid

8 How many new words can you make from the words below?

GREENHOUSE EFFECT

sun

Text acknowledgements
The publishers gratefully acknowledge the permissions granted to reproduce copyright material in the book. Every effort has been made to contact the holders of copyright material, but if any have been inadvertently overlooked, the Publisher will be pleased to make the necessary arrangements at the first opportunity.

Cover illustration: *Alice in Wonderland* Reprinted by permission of HarperCollins*Publishers* Ltd © 2015 Emma Chichester Clark.
Alice in Wonderland Reprinted by permission of HarperCollins*Publishers* Ltd © 2015 Emma Chichester Clark; *Living with Climate Change* Reprinted by permission of HarperCollins*Publishers* Ltd © 2009 Alison Sage.

We are grateful to the following for permission to reproduce copyright material:
Extracts on p.4 from *Saffy's Angel* by Hilary McKay, first published by Hodder Children's Books in 2001, new edition 2021 by Macmillan Children's Books, an imprint of Pan Macmillan, copyright © Hilary McKay, 2001. Reproduced with the permission of Macmillan Publishers International Ltd; Margaret K. McElderry Books, an imprint of Simon & Schuster Children's Publishing Division; and The Bent Agency on behalf of the author. All rights reserved; and an extract on p.43 from *Rainbow Reading Level 5 – Space Workers* by Daphne Paizee, copyright © Cambridge University Press, 2009. Reproduced with permission of the Licensor through PLSclear.

Photo acknowledgements
The publishers wish to thank the following for permission to reproduce photographs. Every effort has been made to trace copyright holders and to obtain their permission for the use of copyright materials. The publishers will gladly receive any information enabling them to rectify any error or omission at the first opportunity.

(t = top, c = centre, b = bottom, r = right, l = left)

p7 top John T Takai/Shutterstock, p9 stockcreations/Shutterstock, p10t Adam Vilimek/Shutterstock, p10b fox_krol/Shutterstock, p13 Teguh Mujiono/Shutterstock, p19 Pontus Edenberg/Shutterstock, p27 Mikhail Tchkheidze/Shutterstock, p35 Christos Georghiou/Shutterstock, p36 Olivier Le Moal/Shutterstock, p45 Tim the Finn/Shutterstock, p49 waniuszka/Shutterstock, p50 JupiterImages/Shutterstock, p51 Quarta/Shutterstock, p52 iralu/Shutterstock, p54 titov dmitriy/Shutterstock, p57t GMB Akash, p57tc Rebecca Nduku, p57c Rafaelle Castera, p57bc Aleksandr Rybalko/Shutterstock, p57b Rebecca Nduku.